A PRACTICAL BOOK OF MEDICINAL CHEMISTRY-I (BP406P)

AS PER NEW PCI SYLLABUS FOR SECOND YEAR B.PHARMACY SEMESTER-IV

PROF. LAHU DINKAR TANDALE

PROF. PRATIKSHA AKSHAY RAHANE

PROF. SACHIN DILIP WAKCHAURE

MR. HANUMANT ARJUN GHULE

I would like to dedicate my work to my family, Friends & my teachers.

They instilled in me a desire to learn and made sacrifices so I would have access to high quality education from an early age.

Also, this is dedicated to my close friends who have always supported me throughout my years of studies.

Prof. Lahu D. Tandale

Prof. Pratiksha A. Rahane

Prof.Sachin D.Wakchaure

Mr. Hanumant A. Ghule

Contents

Foreword

There has always been much interest in the field of pharmaceutical chemistry. Recently, the growth of the field has led to interest by other, non-medical fields. The emphasis of this textbook by Prof. Lahu D. Tandale Prof. Pratiksha A. Rahane, Prof.Sachin D.Wakchaure & Mr. Hanumant A. Ghule is to broadly review the field of pharmaceutical chemistry. This textbook is designed to provide basic information on practical of Medicinal Chemistry to Pharmacy students. Given the broad spectrum of the topic, it is challenging to cover all aspects of Medicinal Chemistry thoroughly, and Lahu Tandale, Pratiksha Rahane, Sachin Wakchaure & Hanumant Ghule has not only managed to provide a text that is thorough but also clear and understandable.

This textbook covers topics ranging from defining basic practical terms to synthesize and explaining synthesis procedures of various compounds. This book will be an excellent reference for anyone interested in the experiments of Medicinal chemistry. This textbook on Medicinal chemistry is practical, informative and enlightening. It presents a topic that is new to many people in a way that is both simple and thorough. It will hopefully bring this important experiments out for people other than in the health care field to see. This book gives new meaning and new insights to those interested in understanding Practical of Medicinal chemistry. It has been a pleasure reading this book and I hope the reader and student will find it as informative as I did.

Prof. Lahu D. Tandale
Prof. Pratiksha A. Rahane
Prof.Sachin D.Wakchaure
Mr. Hanumant A. Ghule

Preface

As per the need of students and instructors, we have been engaged in writing and compiling the data based on Pharmacy Council of India regulated syllabus. It gives us immense pleasure to introduce "Text book of Medicinal Chemistry-II in continuation with "Practical book of Medicinal Chemistry-1". This book has been designed and arranged to provide the basic knowledge of chemistry, classification, mechanism of action and uses of the drugs mentioned in the course of study. The content is focused on synthesis and structure activity relationship of drugs which enable determination of chemical group responsible for evoking a target biological effect in the organism.

The contents of the book are structured as per Pharmacy Council of India regulated syllabus and will be more useful to undergraduate students pursuing carrier in Pharmaceutical Sciences in India.

Book is written in a simple and comprehensive manner along with the structure, schematic diagrams and tables that clearly demonstrate core concept regarding Practical of Medicinal Chemistry. The authentic text of the book will definitely furnish exhaustive information to the students with impressively and user-friendly style.

We will be grateful to all the students, teachers and readers for their constructive suggestions to improve the quality of content of this book. The suggestions from all the readers will be highly appreciated and will be incorporated in the next edition.

Prof. Lahu D. Tandale
Prof. Pratiksha A. Rahane
Prof.Sachin D.Wakchaure
Mr. Hanumant A. Ghule

Acknowledgements

It is a matter of great pride and immense pleasure to extend our sincere regards and deepest sense of gratitude towards Management of Shri Swami Samarth Institute of Pharmacy, Malwadi (Bota) Management team of Matoshri Radha College of Pharmacy Virgaon for their continuous encouragement, constructive criticism and invaluable support for the publication of this book.

It is a pleasure moment for all of us to gratefully acknowledge the constant co-operation of Principals, colleagues and friends of both pharmacy colleges for their inspiration, help and guidance, which provided us confidence during writing of this book.

We cordially acknowledge our family members (Spouse and children) who have not only endured but also encouraged assisted and inspired throughout our writing endeavor.

We express our heartfelt thanks to Dr.Dighe N.S, Dr. Bhawar S.B. Dr. Laware R.B. Dr.Dukre T.P. and other supporting staff members of Pravara, Matoshri Radha College of Pharmacy& SSSIOP Malwadi , for their helpful suggestions and skilful supervision which helped us to mould the text in a beautiful book.

Last but not least, we would like to dedicate this book to our beloved parents, whose love and blessings provided us tremendous emotional support and the zeal to work hard towards our goal.

Prof. Lahu D. Tandale
Prof. Pratiksha A. Rahane
Prof.Sachin D.Wakchaure
Mr. Hanumant A. Ghule

Prologue

We are sharing our knowledge with society.Publishing this book for better clarity in siple ways.
Thank you.......

Safety Instruction

INTRODUCTION TO CHEMICAL HANDLING AND SAFETY IN THE LABORATORY:

1.1 INSTRUCTIONS TO THE STUDENTS:

1. Before entering in the Laboratory:

- One should wear a clean, white Apron.
- Ensure that you are with all the necessary writing material, observation book, calculator, pencil, eraser, requirements box and a neatly covered journal completed in all aspects.

2. While working in the laboratory:

- Maintain discipline and cleanliness. Never lean on the platforms. Follow the instructions given by teacher scrupulously.
- Follow the SOPs correctly while operating the equipments. The log books of sophisticated equipments should be maintained.
- Work cautiously while working with power driven or mobile equipments, gas burners etc.
- Handle acids or other hazardous chemicals carefully. For pipetting such corrosive chemicals, use rubber bulbs "DO NOT SUCK BY MOUTH"
- Do not keep the organic and volatile solvents near the gas flame.
- Also replace the lids on the reagent bottles especially volatile chemicals after use.
- Use only electric water bath for warming any organic solvents.
- "AVOID DIRECT HEATING ORGANIC CHEMICALS UNLESS OTHERWISE DIRECTED"

1.2 FIRST AID TREATMENT IN CASE OF ACCIDENT OR INJURY:

A. BURNS: -

1. Burns caused by Dry Heat (e.g. by Flames, Hot Objects): - For slight burns in which skin is not burnt, apply burnol. For more severe burns, call for medical aid.

2. Acid on the Skin: - Wash immediately and thoroughly with liberal quantity of water, then with saturated sodium bicarbonate solution and finally with water.

3. Alkali on the Skin: - Wash immediately with a large volume of water, then with 1% acetic acid, and finally with water.

4. Bromine on the Skin: - (Serious!) Wash the affected part immediately with cloth/cotton sponge soaked in light petroleum and then rub glycerin well into the skin. After a little while, remove the superficial glycerin and apply burnol.

5. Sodium on the Skin: - If any small fragment of sodium can be seen, remove it carefully with forceps. Wash thoroughly with water, then with 1% acetic acid, finally with water.

6. Organic substance on the skin: - Wash with cotton/cloth soaked in rectified spirit, then with soap and warm water.

B. CUTS: -

- If the cut is only a minor one, allow it to bleed for a few seconds; make sure that no glass particle remains.
- Apply a disinfectant (Rectified Spirit or Dettol) and bandage. For serious cuts, send for a doctor at once: meanwhile wash with a disinfectant and check bleeding by applying pressure immediately above the cut.
- Continuous pressure should not be maintained for more than five minutes.

C. EYE ACCIDENTS: -

In all cases, the patient must see a doctor, if the accident appears serious, medical aid should be summoned immediately while first aid is applied.

1. Acid in the eye,

If the acid is dilute: - Wash the eye repeatedly with 1% sodium bicarbonate solution in the eyecup.

If the acid is concentrated: - First wash the eye with a large amount of water and then continue with the bicarbonate solution.

2. Caustic alkali in the eye: - (Serious!) Proceed as for acid in the eye, but wash with 1 % boric acid solution in place of bicarbonate solution. Do not neglect to consult a Physician.

3. Bromine in the Eye: - (Serious!) Wash thoroughly with water and then immediately with 1% sodium bicarbonate solution.

4. Glass in the Eye: - Remove loose glass very gently with forceps or by washing with water in an eyecup. Call the Doctor Immediately.

D. FIRES: -

- In the event of one's clothing catch fire, the victim should roll over on the ground or should be covered with a fire blanket. Fire extinguisher should not be directly used on a person.
- Inflammable solvents should be handled carefully.

1. Carbon tetrachloride should not be used if sodium or potassium is present as violent explosions may result.

2. The laboratory must be ventilated immediately and well.

3. For burning oil or organic solvents, do not use water, as it will spread the fire. Mixture of sand and sodium bicarbonate is very effective.

E. POISONS: -

Solids or Liquids: -

1. In the mouth but not swallowed: - Spit out at once and wash repeatedly with water.

2. If swallowed: - Call a doctor immediately. In the meanwhile, give an antidote according to the nature of the poison

a) Acids (including oxalic acid): dilute by drinking water, followed by limewater or magnesia.

b) Caustic alkalis: dilute by drinking water, followed by vinegar, lemon or orange juice, or solutions of lactic or citric acid. Milk may then be given but no emetics.

c) Salts of heavy metals: give milk or white of an egg.

d) Arsenic or mercury compound: give an emetic immediately, e.g., one teaspoonful of mustard, or one teaspoonful of salt or zinc sulphate, in a cup of warm water.

F. GAS: -

1. Remove the victim to the open air and loosen clothing at neck. To counteract chlorine or bromine fumes if inhaled in only small amounts, inhale ammonia vapor or gargle with sodium bicarbonate solution.

2. Afterwards, the patient should suck eucalyptus oil-soaked cotton swabs or drink warm dilute peppermint or cinnamon essence to smoothen the throat and lungs.

3. If breathing has stopped, apply artificial respiration.

Call for Medical AID Immediately.

1.3 CARE IN CHEMISTRY LABORATORY:

- Benches should always be kept clean and tidy. All the spillages of both solids and liquids must be cleared away immediately.
- All glassware must be scrupulously cleaned.
- Under no circumstances should be working surface of the bench become cluttered with apparatus.
- All apparatus associated with one particular operation should be grouped together on the bench.
- If a solution, precipitate, filtrate, etc, is set aside for subsequent, the container must be labeled so that contents can be readily identified.
- Regent bottles must be replaced on the regent shelves immediately after use.
- Normal practice is that all determinations are performed in duplicate.
- A stiff covered notebook of A 4 size must be provided for recording experimental observations as they made.
- Fire extinguisher must be placed handy in every chemical laboratory

1.4 SAFETY:

Safety in the laboratory is essential at all times. You are responsible for the safety of any other person as well as your own. Many chemicals encountered in analysis are poisonous and must be carefully handled. The more precaution is to be taken for concentrated acids, poisons such as potassium cyanide, halogenated

solvents, benzene, and mercury. Many operations involving chemical reactions are potentially dangerous and recommended procedures must be followed and obeyed. All laboratory workers/person should familiarize themselves with local safety requirements, which may include the compulsory wearing of lab coats and safety spectacles, and the positions of first aid equipment.

1.5 THE GRADES AND PROPERTIES OF CHEMICALS:

In the analytical chemistry, accuracy of analysis is affected by the principal factor viz the quality of the regents. The chemicals, which are used in the laboratory for chemicals analysis, are available indifferent grades as follows.

    1. **Technical or Commercial Grade:** -These are used when the high purity is not required e.g. preparation of cleaning solution. For this potassium dichromate and sulphuric acid are required.

2. **Chemically pure (CP Grade):**- These are more refined than the technical grade. These chemicals are not suitable for analytical work or if, to be used, they must be tested.

3. **L.R. Grade:** - These are used for analytical work. Its label indicates maximum limits of impurities allowed by the specifications, or actual results of analysis for various impurities.

4. **Primary standard:** - These are in the purest form, carefully analyzed and the assay value (percentage purity) is printed on the label.

5. **Pharmacopoeial Grade Chemicals:** - These chemicals confirm the tolerances set by pharmacopoeias. (Ex. Indian pharmacopoeia & British Pharmacopoeia)

1.6 CARE IN HANDILING OF CHEMICALS:

Handling of chemicals specially hazards chemicals must be done with due care. Everyday working in the laboratory must follow certain rules while handling the chemicals. Select the required grade of the chemical for the analytical work. Select the smallest pack as available. Replace the top of every container immediately after removal of reagent; do not rely on someone to do this. Use clean spatula for removing the chemical reagent from the container. Observe the special instruction if any mentioned on the container. Remove the required amount of chemical reagent from the container, so there is no need of returning excess to container, so as to avoid the contamination of product. Keep the reagent and the laboratory balances clean. Clean any spilled chemicals immediately. While handling hazardous or toxic chemicals use hand gloves and mouth mask.

1.7 LABELING OF LABORATORY REAGENTS:

Hazard Symbols: Legends on packaging and labeling of dangerous substances define hazardous chemicals under the following categories:

    Corrosive: These products may destroy living tissue; eyes are particularly susceptible; Emergency showers should be available. If swallowed, plenty of water should be given after immediate mouth rinsing

    Toxic: These products can cause death or serious illness when small amounts enter the body by ingestion, inhalation of vapor, fumes or dust, or by absorption through the skin; hygiene considerations should be rigorously observed.

    Oxidizing: These compounds may cause fire and will always assist combustion. They produce heat on contact with organic matter and reducing agents.

    Explosive: These products may explode by the action of heat, sources of ignition, shock or friction. The compounds are often packaged wet to reduce the risk of explosion; they will become dangerous if allowed to dry. Some compounds form sensitive explosive salts on contact with metals.

Flammable: These compounds have a low flash point, and those which react with water or damp air to give rise to flammable gases (e.g. hydrogen) from metal hydrides. Ignition sources include Bunsen burners, hot metal surfaces, electric sparks, etc. Fire fighting equipments should be readily available and frequently checked.

Harmful: Irritant chemicals cause inflammation of the skin, mucous membranes, or discomfort of the respiratory system. All laboratory chemicals should be regarded as harmful; some are specifically harmful by skin contact, inhalation or swallowing.

Syllabus

I) Preparation of Drugs/ Intermediate

1. 1,3-pyrazole
2. Oxazole derivative
3. Benzimidazole
4. Benzotriazole
5. 2,3-diphenyl quinoxaline
6. Benzocaine
7. Phenytoin
8. Phenothiazine
9. Barbiturate

II) Assay of Drugs

1. Chlorpromazine
2. Phenobarbitone
3. Atropine
4. Ibuprofen
5. Aspirin
6. Furosemide

(III) Determination of Partition Coefficient for any two drugs

1. The partition coefficient of succinic acid between ether and water
2. Determination of partition coefficient of benzoic acid between benzene and water.

CHAPTER ONE

EXPERIMENT NO.01

Aim: To Synthesize 5-Methyl-2-(3-nitrophenyl)-1,2-dihydropyrazol-3- one.

Requirements:

Chemicals: 3-Nitro phenyl hydrazine, ethyl acetoacetate, absolute ethanol, chloroform.

Apparatus: Beaker, round bottom fiask, condenser, Buchner funnel, beaker, glass rod, measuring cylinder, filter paper, thermometer

Mechanism:

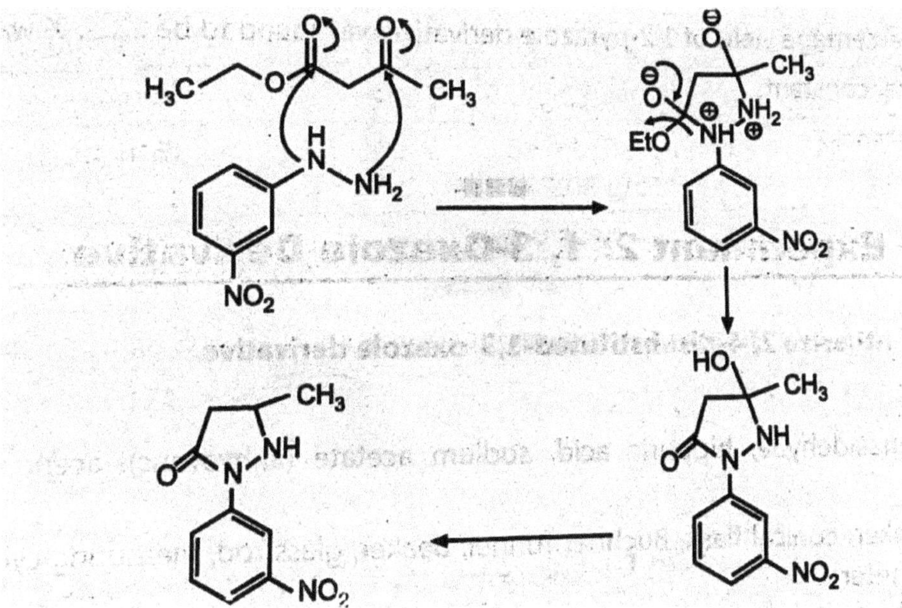

Mechanism

Procedure:

- Dissolve 1.53 g (0.01 mole) of 3-Nitrophenyl hydrazine in 15 mL of absolute ethanol in a 250 mL round bottom flask.
- To this solution, add 7.8 mL (0.05 mole) of ethyl acetoacetate, previously dissolved in
- 15 mL of absolute ethanol.
- Reflux reaction mixture for 3 to 4 hours.
- Distil off excess of ethanol and dissolve residue in 25 mL. chloroform.
- Transfer this chloroform in separating funnel and add 25 mL of water in to it.
- Shake the funnel and separate chloroform layer and evaporate the solvent on water bath in petri plate to yield product.

- Recrystallization: It can be recrystallized from absolute alcohol.

Calculation:
Here limiting reagent is Diphenyl hydrazone; hence yield should be calculated from its amount taken.
Molecular formula of Diphenyl hydrazone = C13H12N2
Molecular formula of 1,3-diphenyl-1H-pyrazole = C15H12N2
Molecular Weight of Diphenyl hydrazone = 196 g/mole
Molecular Weight of 1,3-diphenyl-1H-pyrazole = 220 g/mole
Theoretical yield:
196 g Diphenyl hydrazone forms 220 g 1,3-diphenyl-1H-pyrazole
Therefore, 0.91 g Diphenyl hydrazone will form......(X) g 1,3-diphenyl-1H-pyrazole X = (220×0.91)/196 = 1.02 g
Theoretical yield = 1.02 g
Practical Yield=.........
Practical Yield
Percentage (%) Yield = ---------------------------- × 100
Theoretical yield
Percentage yield = __________%
Report:

- 5-Methyl-2-(3-nitrophenyl)-1,2-dihydropyrazol-3-one preapred and submitted.
- The percentage yield was found to be __________________.

CHAPTER TWO

EXPERIMENT No.02

AIM: To Synthesis of 4-benzylidene-2-phenyl oxazole-5-one

REQUIREMENTS:

Chemicals: Glycine, Sodium hydroxide, Benzoyl chloride, Concentrated hydrochloric acid, Benzaldehyde, Acetic anhydride, Anhydrous sodium acetate, Ethanol.

Apparatus: Round bottom flask, Reflux condenser, Beaker, Glass rod, Funnel, Measuring cylinder.

PRINCIPLE & MECHANISM:

The principle involved in the preparation of 4-benzylidene-2-phenyl oxazole-5-one is dehydration followed by cyclization method. The active methylene group react with aromatic aldehydes. Benzoyl glycine reacts with benzaldehyde followed by dehydration gives 4- benzylidene-2-phenyl oxazole-5-one. The hippuric acid is formed by reacting glycine with benzoyl chloride.

Procedure:

- About 1 gm of glycine was dissolved in aqueous sodium hydroxide solution (10 ml) in a flask and to it 1.5 ml of benzoyl chloride was added.
- The mouth of the flask was plugged with cotton and was shaken vigorously. Then 1-2 drops of conc. HCl was added. The product was filtered, washed with water and recrystallized.
- A mixture of benzaldehyde, benzoyl glycine, acetic anhydride and anhydrous sodium acetate was taken in a conical flask and the contents were heated on sand/oil bath till the mixture had liquified completely.
- Now, the contents were heated on a water bath for two hours.

- Then it was cooled, and to it 25 ml ethanol was added slowly.
- The product was filtered, washed with hot water, dried, and recrystallized.

Calculation:
Molecular formula of 4-benzylidene-2-phenyl oxazole-5-one =
Molecular formula of Benzoyl glycine =
Molecular weight of 4-benzylidene-2-phenyl oxazole-5-one =
Molecular weight of Benzoyl glycine =
Theoretical yield:
.... gm of Benzoyl glycine forms ...... gm 4-benzylidene-2-phenyl oxazole-5-one. Therefore, ... gm Benzoyl glycine will form.........(X) gm 4-benzylidene-2-phenyl oxazole- 5-one.
Theoretical yield = ...
Practical Yield=..........
Practical Yield
Percentage (%) Yield = ---------------------------- × 100
Theoretical yield
Percentage yield = __________%
REPORT:

- 4-benzylidene-2-phenyl oxazole-5-one was prepared and submitted.
- The percentage yield was found to be __________________.

CHAPTER THREE

EXPERIMENT NO.03

Aim: To prepare and submit Benzimidazole from o-phenylenediamine.

Reqiurement:

Chemicals: o-phenylenediamine, Formic acid, NaOH

Apparatus: Beaker, conical flask, measuring jar, water bath etc.,

Principle:

The principle involved in the synthesis of Benzimidazole is Phillips reaction involves the condensation of ortho phenylenediamines with organic acids in presence of dilute mineral acids to furnish Benzimidazoles.

Mechanism:

Initially one of the amino groups is acylated with the organic acid in presence of mineral acid to furnish an N-acylated compound. In the next step, the other nitrogen is also acylated by making bond with the carbonyl carbon of the first acyl group leading to ring closure.

benzimidazole reaction & Mechanism

Procedure:

- Placed 27g of O-phenylenediamine in a round bottomed flask of 250ml and added 17.5g
- (16ml) of 90% formic acid. Heated the mixture on a water bath at 1000C for 2 hour.

- Cooled and added 10% sodium hydroxide solution slowly, with constant rotation of the flask, until the mixture is just alkaline to litmus.
- Filter off the synthesized crude benzimidazole by using the pump wash with ice cold water.
- Recyrstallisation: Dissolved the synthesized product in 400ml of boiling water, added 2g of decolorizing carbon and digest for 15minutes.
- Filter rapidly through Buchner funnel and a flask at the pump. Cool the filtrate to about 100C, filter off the benzimidazole, wash with 25ml of cold water and dry at 100^0 C.
- The yield of pure benzimidazole is 25g (85%), m.p 171-172^0 C .

CALCULATION

Here limiting reagent is O-phenylene diamine; hence yield should be calculated from its amount taken.

Molecular formula of O-phenylene diamine = C6H8N2

Molecular formula of benzimidazole = C7H6N2

Molecular weight of O-phenylene diamine = 108g/mole

Molecular weight of benzilidazole = 118g/mole

108g of O-phenylene diamine forms 118g benzimidazole

Therefore, 27g O-phenylene diamine will form.........(X) g benzimidazole

X = (118 X 27)/108 = 29.5g

Theoretical yield = 29.5g

Practical yield = ... g

$$\text{Percentage (\%) Yield} = \frac{\text{Practical Yield}}{\text{Theoretical yield}} \times 100$$

Percentage yield = __________%

Report:

- Benzimidazole was synthesized from O-phenylene diamine and submitted.
- The percentage yield was found to be _________________.

CHAPTER FOUR

EXPERIMENT NO.04

Aim: To synthesize and submit benzotriazole from o-phenylene diamine

Reqiurement:

Chemicals: o-phenylenediamine, glacial acetic acid, sodium nitrite

Apparatus: Beaker, round bottom fiask, condenser, Buchner funnel, beaker, glass rod, measuring cylinder, filter paper, thermometer

Principle:

The sodium nitrite reacts with glacial acetic acid and liberates nitrous acid. The o-phenylene diamine reacts with nitrous acid and produce diazonium ion. When the structure and stereochemistry of diazonium ion are stable, intramolecular nitrogen coupling occurs and form benzotriazole directly.

Mechanism:

benzotriazole mechanism

Procedure:

- Dissolve 1.3g of o-phenylenediamine in a mixture of 1.5ml of glacial acetic acid and 5ml water in a beaker.
- Stir until the solid dissolves, warm gently if necessary. Cool the solution to 15 C. Stir well and add a solution of 2g of sodium nitrite in 2ml water.
- Reaction mixture become warm within 2-3 minutes and reaches a temperature of about 850C and then begins to cool.
- Colour changes from deep red to pale brown. Continue stirring for 15 minutes till the temperature fall about $35\text{-}40^0$ C.
- Thoroughly chill in ice bath for 30 minutes. Filter the product and wash with cold water.

calculations:

Molecular weight of o-phenylene diamine =
Molecular weight of benzotriazole =
---- g of o-phenylene diamine gives ----- g of benzotriazole
1g of o-phenylene diamine =
    Theoretical yield =..........
Practical yield =...............
    Practical Yield

Percentage (%) Yield = ----------------------------- × 100
Theoretical yield
    Percentage yield = __________%
    REPORT:

- Benzotriazole was prepared and submitted.
- The percentage yield was found to be ________________.

CHAPTER FIVE

EXPERIMENT NO.05

Aim: To synthesize and submit 2,3-diphenyl quinoxaline from o-phenylenediamine and report its percentage yield.

Requirement:

Chemicals: o-phenylenediamine, benzil, rectified spirit.

Apparatus: Beaker, conical flask, measuring jar, water bath etc.,

Principle :

Quinoxalines are a type of heterocyclic compounds. They are also known as benzopyrazines.

benzopyrazine

pyrazine

Generally quinoxaline is formed by the condensation of o-phenylenediamine with diketones. Here 2,3-diphenyl quinoxaline is prepared by treating o-phenylenediamine with benzil.

o-phenylene diamine

benzil

2,3,-diphenyl quinoxaline

Reaction of 2,3 diphenyl quinoxaline

Procedure:

- Add a solution of 1.1g of o-phenylenediamine in 8ml rectified spirit to a warm solution of 2.1g of benzil in 8ml rectified spirit.
- Warm the mixture for 30 minutes in a water bath.
- Add water dropwise until slight cloudiness persists.
- Cool the solution and filter the product.

Calculation:

Molecular weight of 2, 3-diphenyl quinoxaline =

Molecular weight of o-phenylene diamine =

----- g of o-phenylene diamine gives ----- g of 2, 3-diphenyl quinoxaline

1g of o-phenylene diamine =

----- g of o-phenylene diamine =

Theoretical yield =.........

Practical Yield=.........

$$\text{Percentage (\%) Yield} = \frac{\text{Practical Yield}}{\text{Theoretical yield}} \times 100$$

Percentage yield = __________%

REPORT:

- 2,3-diphenyl quinoxaline was prepared and submitted.
- The percentage yield was found to be __________________.

CHAPTER SIX

EXPERIMENT NO.06

AIM: To synthesize benzocaine from para amino benzoic acid.

REQUIREMENTS:

Chemicals: p-amino benzoic acid, Absolute ethanol, concentrated sulfuric acid, Sodium bicarbonate.

Apparatus: Round bottom flask, Beaker, Conical flask, Measuring cylinder, Funnel

PRINCIPLE & MECHANISM:

Aromatic esters are prepared by esterification of aromatic acids with alcohol in the presence of an Conc. H2SO4 or dry HCl which fastens the reaction. Benzocaine is an ester which was prepared by esterification of PABA with ethanol in presence of HCl.

Procedure:

- Place 80ml of absolute ethanol in a 250-ml two-necked flask equipped with a double surface reflux condenser and a gas inlet tube.
- Pass dry hydrogen chloride through the alcohol until saturated.
- The increase in weight is about 20gm, remove the gas inlet tube, introduce 12gm of paminobenzoic acid and heat the mixture under reflux for 2 hours.
- Upon cooling, the reaction mixture sets to a solid mass of the hydrochloride of ethyl p- aminobenzoate.
- It is better, however, to pour the hot solution into 30 ml of water (no hydrochloride separates) and add solid sodium carbonate carefully to the clear solution until it is neutral to litmus.
- Filter off the precipitated ester at the pump and dry in the air.

Calculation:

Molecular formula of Benzocaine =

Molecular formula of p-amino benzoic acid =

Molecular weight of Benzocaine =

Molecular weight of p-amino benzoic acid =

Theoretical yield:

-----gm of p-amino benzoic acid gives ----- gm of Benzocaine.

Therefore, ... gm p-amino benzoic acid will form .... (X) gm Benzocaine.

Theoretical yield =..........

Practical Yield=.........

Practical Yield

Percentage (%) Yield = ----------------------------- × 100

Theoretical yield

Percentage yield = __________%

REPORT:

- Benzocaine was prepared and submitted.
- The percentage yield was found to be _________________.

CHAPTER SEVEN

Experiment No.07

AIM: To prepare and submit phenytoin from benzoin and urea.

REQUIREMENTS:

Chemicals: Urea, Nitric acid, Benzoin, Sodium hydroxide, ethanol, conc:HCl

Apparatus: Round bottom flask ,reflex condenser, funnel, beaker, filter paper, glass rod.

PRINCIPLE & MECHANISM:

Phenytoin is 5,5-diphenyl imidazoline 2,4-dione.Benzil react with urea in the presence of alkali and alcohol to give phenytoin by pinacolone rearrangement.

Principle of phenytoin

Mechanism:

PROCEDURE:

- Place 5.3 g (0.025 mol) of benzil, 3.0 g (0.05 mol) of urea, 15 ml of aqueous sodium hydroxide solution (30%) and 75 ml of ethanol in a round bottomed flask of 100 ml capacity.
- Set up a reflux condenser with the flask and boil using an electric heating mantle for at least 2 h.
- Cool to room temperature, pour the reaction mixture into 125 ml of water and mix carefully.
- Allow the reaction mixture to stand for 15 min and then filter the product under suction to remove an insoluble by-product.
- Render the filtrate strongly acidic with concentrated hydrochloric acid, cool in ice-water and immediately filter off the precipitated product under suction.
- Recrystallise at least once from industrial spirit to obtain about 2.8 g (44%) of pure 5,5-diphenylhydantoin, m.p. 297-298 °C.

CALCULATION:

Here limiting reagent is benzil; hence yield should be calculated from its amount taken.

Molecular formula of benzil =

Molecular formula of phenytoin =

Molecular weight of benzil =

Molecular weight of phenytoin =

Theoretical Yield:

________ g benzil forms ________ g phenytoin

Theoretical Yield=

Practical Yield=………

$$\text{Percentage (\%) Yield} = \frac{\text{Practical Yield}}{\text{Theoretical yield}} \times 100$$

Percentage yield = _________ %

REPORT:

- Phenytoin was prepared and submitted.
- The percentage yield was found to be __________________.

CHAPTER EIGHT

EXPERIMENT NO.08

AIM: To Prepare and submit Phenothiazine from diphenylamine

REQUIREMENTS:

Chemicals:

Apparatus: Round bottom flask ,reflex condenser, funnel, beaker, filter paper, glass rod.

PRINCIPLE :

Diphenylamine undergoes cyclization reaction with sulphur and anhydrous aluminium chloride at 140-150°C and forms a melted mass with the evolution of hydrogen sulphide gas. Further the melted mass is extracted with distilled water and followed by dilute alcohol pure phenothiazine separates out a residue.

PROCEDURE:

* 22 g of diphenylamine, 8.2 g of sulfur, and 3.2 gms. of anhydrous calcium chloride are melted together.
* The reaction sets 140-150° C with the rapid evolution of hydrogen sulfide; by lowering the temperature, a few degrees the reaction can be slackened. When the reaction has moderated, the temperature is raised to 160° C for a time.
* The melt, when cool, is ground up and extracted, first with water and then with dilute alcohol.
* The residue consists of almost pure phenothiazine. It can be recrystallized from alcohol. M.P. 180° C.

CALCULATION:

Molecular formula of Diphenylamine =

Molecular formula of Phenothiazine =

Molecular weight of Diphenylamine =

Molecular weight of Phenothiazine =

Theoretical yield:

.... gm of diphenylamine gives .... gm of Phenothiazine.

Therefore, ... gm diphenylamine will form .... (X) gm Phenothiazine

Theoretical yield = ...

Practical yeild=........

Practical Yield

$$\text{Percentage (\%) Yield} = \frac{\text{Practical Yield}}{\text{Theoretical yield}} \times 100$$

Percentage yield =________ %

REPORT:

- Phenothiazine was prepared and submitted.
- The percentage yield was found to be ________________.

CHAPTER NINE

Experiment No.09

AIM: To prepare barbituric acid from urea and dimethyl malonate.

REQUIREMENTS:

Chemicals: Sodium metal, Ethanol, Diethyl malonate, Urea, Calcium chloride,conc. HC

Apparatus: RBF, Beaker, Measuring cylinder, Reflux condenser, Water bath, Funnel, etc.,

PRINCIPLE & MECHANISM:

Barbituric acid are usually synthesized by carrying out the condensation of either diethyl malonate or its respective alkylated derivatives with urea in the critical presence of a base. Therefore, the interaction of diethyl malonate with urea in the presence of sodium ethoxide perceptively results in the formation of hydro-2,4,6-Trioxo pyrimidine. Barbituric acid may be gainfully utilized in the preparation of its various structural analogues.

Diethyl malonate Urea Barbituric acid

Reaction

Diethyl malonate Urea Barbituric acid

Mechanism

PROCEDURE:

- In a 2-litre round bottomed flask, fitted with a double surface reflux condenser, 11.5 gm of clean sodium was placed.
- Then, 250 ml of absolute ethanol was added in one portion.
- Then, 80 gm of diethyl malonate was added, followed by a solution of 30 gm of dry urea in 250 ml of hot absolute ethanol.
- The mixture was shaken well, fitted with a calcium chloride guard- tube to the top of the condenser and the mixture was refluxed for 7 hours in an oil bath heated to 110^0 CC.
- A white solid separated out. The reaction mixture was treated with 450 ml of hot water and then with concentrated hydrochloric acid, with stirring, until the solution was acid.
- The xresulting solution was filtered and left in the refrigerator overnight.
- The solid was filtered at the pump, washed with 25 ml of cold water, drained well and then dried at 100^0 C for 4 hours.

Calculation:

Molecular formula of Diethyl malonate =

Molecular formula of Barbituric acid =

Molecular weight of Diethyl malonate =

Molecular weight of Barbituric acid =

Theoretical yield:

.... gm of Diethyl malonate gives ....gm of Barbituric acid.

Therefore, ... gm Diethyl malonate will form .... (X) gm Barbituric acid

Theoretical yield = ...

Practical Yield=.........

Practical Yield

Percentage (%) Yield = ----------------------------- × 100

Theoretical yield

Percentage yield = __________%

REPORT:

- Barbituric acid was prepared and submitted.
- The percentage yield was found to be ___________________.

CHAPTER TEN

EXPERIMENT NO.10

AIM: To perform the assay of Chlorpromazine hydrochloride

REQUIREMENTS:

Chemicals: Perchloric acid, Glacial acetic acid, Acetone, Mercuric acetate, Chlorpromazine hydrochloride, Crystal violet, Methyl orange, Potassium hydrogen phthalate.

Apparatus: Measuring cylinder, Conical flask, Volumetric flask, Burette, Beaker

PRINCIPLE :

Chlorpromazine is estimated by non-aqueous titration which is suitable for titration of weak acid and weak base. In this non aqueous solvent like perchloric acid is utilized as a titrant and methyl orange is used as an indicator. Mercuric acetate is added in the non-aqueous titration in order to remove the chloride ions. So as to prevent the interference of the chloride ion released by the titrant. The mercuric acetate replaces the halide ion in chlorpromazine with acetate ion which is a strong base. The end point is indicated by appearance of blue colour.

Chlorpromazine Hydrochloride

Procedure:

Standardization of 0.1 M perchloric acid solution

0.5 gm of potassium hydrogen phthalate was dissolved in 25 ml of glacial acetic acid and few drops of crystal violet indicator was added. The solution was titrated with 0.1 M $HClO_4$ till blue green colour appears.

Assay of Chlorpromazine hydrochloride

Accurately about 0.6 gm was weighed out, dissolved in 200 ml of acetone and 15 ml of mercuric acetate solution was added to it. Titration was carried out with 0.1 M perchloric acid, using a saturated solution of methyl orange in acetone as indicator. A blank titration was also carried out.

1 ml of 0.1 M perchloric acid is equivalent to 0.03553 g of $C_{17}H_{19}ClN_2S$, HCl.

Calculation:

Standardization of 0.1 M $HClO_4$ solution:

Molarity =

Assay of Chlorpromazine:

% purity of Chlorpromazine hydrochloride =

Result:

The percentage purity of Chlorpromazine hydrochloride was found to be =

CHAPTER ELEVEN

EXPERIMENT NO.11

AIM: To perform the Assay of Phenobarbitone.

REQUIREMENTS:

Chemicals: Sodium hydroxide, aldehyde free ethanol, benzoic acid, thymolphthalein solution, silver nitrate, pyridine and ether

Apparatus: Erlenmeyer flask, Volumetric flask, Pipette, Burette etc.,

PRINCIPLE:

Phenobarbitone is assayed by non-aqueous titration.In this method,drug is dissolved in the pyridine and titrated with sodium hydroxide solution using thymolphthalein as an indicator.

Phenobarbitone	Sodium hydroxide	Phenobarbitone sodium

$+ \ 2NaOH \longrightarrow \quad + 2H_2O$

PROCEDURE:

A) STANDARDISATION OF SODIUM HYDROXIDE SOLUTION

Actually weighed 0.6g of benzoic acid and dissolved it in a mixture of 30ml of ethanol and 6ml of water and titrated with ethanolic sodium hydroxide solution using 0.2ml of thymolphthalein as indicator.

B) ASSAY OF PHENOBARBITONE

Weighed and powdered 20 tablets. Weighed a quantity of the powder containing aboutC0.1g (100 mg) of phenobarbitone in 5ml of pyridine add 0.25 ml of thymolphthaleinCsolution and 10 ml of silver nitrate pyridine reagent and titrated with 0.1M ethanolic sodium hydroxide until a pure blue colour is obtained. Repeated the operation without the substance under examination. The difference between the titrations represents the amount of sodium hydroxide required.

Equivalent factor: 1ml of 0.1M ethanolic sodium hydroxide=0.01161g of C12H12N2O3

CALCULATION:

a) Standardization of 0.1M Sodium hydroxide solution

$$\text{Molarity of NaOH} = \frac{\text{Weight (W)}}{\text{Mol. wt of benzoic acid (122.12) X Volume (V)}}$$

Where,

W = Weight of benzoic acid (g)

V = Volume of NaOH solution consumed

a) Determination of Phenobarbitone

$$\text{\% purity of phenobarbitone} = \frac{0.01161 \text{ x V X Molarity (Calculated)}}{\text{Molarity (given) x W}} \text{ X } 100$$

Where,

Molarity (calculated) = Molarity obtained from step (a)

V = Volume of Sodium hydroxide used

0.01161 is the equivalent factor

Molarity (given) = 0.1M

W = weight of sample

Result:

The percentage purity of Phenobarbitone was found to be =

CHAPTER TWELVE

EXPERIMENT NO.12

AIM: To perform the assay of Atropine Sulphate.

REQUIREMENTS:

Chemicals: Atropine sulphate, Potassium hydrogen phthalate, Perchloric acid, Glacial acetic acid, Crystal violet

Apparatus: Measuring cylinder, Conical flask, Volumetric flask, Burette, Beaker

PRINCIPLE :

Atropine is assayed by non-aqueous titration which is generally used for the titration of weak acid with weak base. In this titration non-aqueous solvent (perchloric acid) and crystal violet solution is used as an indicator. At the end point blue colour is obtained.

Atropine Sulphate

Procedure:

Standardization of 0.1 M perchloric acid solution

0.5 gm of potassium hydrogen phthalate was dissolved in 25 ml of glacial acetic acid and few drops of crystal violet indicator was added. The solution was titrated with 0.1 M HClO4 till blue green colour appears.

Assay of Atropine Sulphate

Accurately about 0.5g was weighed out and dissolved in 30 ml of anhydrous glacial acetic acid. Titration was carried out with 0.1 M perchloric acid and the end point was determined potentiometrically. A blank titration was also carried out.

1 ml of 0.1M perchloric acid is equivalent to 0.06768 g of (C17H23NO3), H2SO4.

Calculation:

Standardization of 0.1 M HClO4 solution:

Molarity =

Assay of Atropine Sulphate:

% purity of Atropine Sulphate =

Result:

The percentage purity of atropine sulphate was found to be =

CHAPTER THIRTEEN

Experiment No.13

AIM: To perform the assay of Ibuprofen.

REQUIREMENTS:

Chemicals: Ibuprofen, Sodium hydroxide, Phenolphthalein, Ethanol, Oxalic acid

Apparatus: Burette, Conical flask, Volumetric flask, Bulb pipette, Beaker, Funnel

PRINCIPLE:

The principle involoved in the assay of Ibuprofen is acid-base titration where the acidic group in Ibuprofen is neutralized by titrating with base i.e. NaOH using phenolphthalein as an indicator where the end point is colourless to pink

Ibuprofen

Procedure:

Standardization of sodium hydroxide solution:

Weigh about 0.5gm of KHP into 250-mL Erlenmeyer flask which was previously powdered and dried at 1100C. Dissolve the sample in about 30 mL of distilled water before you titrate. Add five drops of phenolphthalein indicator and titrate with 0.1M NaOH by constant swirling to the first appearance of a permanent pink color.

Each mL of 0.1M NaOH is equivalent to 0.02042gm of C8H5KO4.

Assay of ibuprofen:

Weigh accurately about 0.5gm of drug and dissolve in 100ml of ethanol (95%) and titrate with a 0.1m NaOH using phenolphthalein as an indicator where the end point is permanent pink colour. Repeat the titration with blank.

Each mL of 0.1M NaOH is equivalent to 0.02663gm of C13H18O2.

Titre value x molarity of NaOH x Eq. factor

% purity of phenobarbitone = --- X 100

Weight taken x expected molarity

Result:

The percentage purity of Ibuprofen was found to be=

CHAPTER FOURTEEN

Experiment No.14

AIM: To determine percentage purity of Aspirin.

  REQUIREMENTS:

  Chemicals: Aspirin, sodium hydroxide, Potassium hydrogen phthalate, Phenolphthalein indicator, Phenol red etc.,

  Apparatus: Erlenmeyer flask, Volumetric flask, Pipette, Burette etc.,

  PRINCIPLE:

The principle involved in the assay of Aspirin is acid base titration where theacidic group in aspirin is neutralized by titrating with base i.e. NaOH and the excess base is back titrated with an acid (HCl) using phenol red as an indicator where the end point is pink to colourless.

ASPIRIN

  Procedure:

Standardization of 0.5 M NaOH:

  Weigh about 2.5gm of KHP into 250-mL Erlenmeyer flask which was previously powdered and dried at 1100C. Dissolve the sample in about 30 mL of distilled water before you titrate. Add five drops of phenolphthalein indicator and titrate with 0.5M NaOH by constant swirling to the first appearance of a permanent pink color.

  Each mL of 0.5M NaOH is equivalent to 0.1021gm of C8H5KO4.

  Standardization of 0.5M HCl:

Pipette out 20 mL of 0.5m NaOH solution into 250mL Erlenmeyer flask and add five drops of phenolphthalein indicator and titrate with 0.5M HCl by constant swirling to the disappearance of pink color.

  Assay of aspirin:

  Weigh accurately about 0.5 gm of sample dissolved in 15m: of ethanol (95%), add 50mL of 0.5M NaOH. Boil gently for 10 minutes, cool and titrate the excess alkali with 0.5M HCl using Phenol red as an indicator. Repeat the titration with blank.

  Each mL of 0.5M HCl is equivalent to 0.04504gm of C9H7O4.

$$\% \text{ purity of aspirin} = \frac{\text{Titre value x molarity of NaOH x Eq. factor}}{\text{Weight taken x expected molarity}} \times 100$$

Result:

The percentage purity of aspirin was found to be=

CHAPTER FIFTEEN

EXPERIMENT NO.15

AIM: To carry out the Assay of furosemide tablets.

REQUIREMENTS:

Chemicals: Furosemide, dimethyl formamide, sodium hydroxide, bromothymol blue indicator,0.1N oxalic acid, Phenolphthalein indicator

Apparatus: Measuring cylinder, Conical flask, Volumetric flask, Burette, Beaker,Erlenmeyer flask.

PRINCIPLE:

It is assayed by aqueous acid base titration between weak acid furosemide and strong alkali sodium hydroxide. In this assay protophilic solvent dimethyl formamide is used which enhances the acidity of furosemide so that it can be titrated with sodium hydroxide. To make theeffect of acid impurities present negligible a solvent blank determination is carried out.

Furosemide

PREPARATION AND STANDARDIZATION OF STANDARD SOLUTIONS

a) Standardization of 0.1m sodium hydroxide solution

Solutions of any molarity xM may be prepared by dissolving 40x g of Sodium hydroxide in sufficient water to produce 1000ml.

b) Standardization of 0.1m sodium hydroxide solution

Weighed accurately about 5g of potassium hydrogen phthalate previously dried at 1200C for two hours dissolve in 75ml of carbon dioxide free water. Added 0.1ml of phenolphthalein solution and titrate with the sodium hydroxide until a permanent pink color is produced.

Each ml of 0.1M NaOH equivalent to 0.02042g of potassium hydrogen phthalate.

PROCEDURE:

a) Assay method by (neutralization titration)

Weighed and powdered 20 tablets and weighed accurately about a quantity of powder equivalent to 0.5g and dissolve in 40ml of dimethyl formamide and titrate with 0.1M sodium hydroxide using bromothymol blue as an indicator the end point shows the colour change from yellow to blue. Carry out a blank titration.

b) Assay method by (uv spectrophotometry)

Weighed and powdered 20 tablets and weigh accurately about a quantity of powder equivalent to 0.1g of furosemide and shake with 150ml of 0.1M sodium hydroxide for 10 minutes. Added sufficient 0.1M sodium hydroxide to produce 250ml and filter. Dilute 5ml to 200ml with 0.1M sodium hydroxide and measure the absorbance of the resulting solution at the maximum at about 271nm.Calculate the content of $C_{12}H_{11}ClN_2O_5S$ taking 580 as the value of A (1%, 1cm) at the maximum at about 271 nm.

Result:

The given sample contains .... mg of furosemide.

CHAPTER SIXTEEN

EXPERIMENT NO.16

AIM: The partition coefficient of succinic acid between ether and water

REQUIREMENTS:

Chemicals: Succinic acid, Ether, Phenolphthalein, Sodium hydroxide

Apparatus: Beaker, Measuring cylinder, Volumetric flask, Separating funnel

PRINCIPLE:

When an excess amount of solid or liquid is added to a mixture of two immiscible liquids while this substance is slightly soluble in both immiscible liquids. It will distribute itself between the two phases until saturation if mixed by shaking vigorously. If the insufficient amount of substance is added in two immiscible liquids to the saturation, it gets distributed in two layer at a definite ratio, this phenomenon is called as distribution law or partition law. The ratio constant is called as partition coefficient or distribution coefficient. It is independent of the total amount of the substance dissolved.

$$K = \frac{C_1}{C_2}$$

Where, K is a constant known as distribution or partition coefficient. C1 and C2 are the concentration of a solute in the two immiscible liquids.

Procedure:

A solution of succinic acid in water was prepared. Then, 30 ml, 40 ml, and 50 ml of this solution was transferred in three stoppered flask. To it, 20 ml and 10 ml of water was added to make total 50 ml. Then, 50 ml of ether was added, shaken vigorously and each flask was allowed to stay at constant thermostatic temperature. The two layers were then separated out. 10 ml of ether layer was pipetted out and to it 25 ml of water, phenolphthalein indicator was added and titrated with 0.05 N sodium hydroxide solution. The procedure was then repeated with the aqueous layer.

Observation table:

Volume of 0.05 N NaOH consumed		
	Ether layer	**Aqueous layer**
Flask 1		
Flask 2		
Flask 3		

Determination of K values

Sl. No	C ether	C aqueous	$K = C_{ether}/C_{aqueous}$
Flask 1			
Flask 2			
Flask 3			

Result:

The partition co-efficient between ether & water was found to be.......................... .

CHAPTER SEVENTEEN

EXPERIMENT NO.17

AIM: Determination of partition coefficient of benzoic acid between benzene and water.

REQUIREMENTS:

Chemicals: solution of benzoic acid in benzene,benzene,0.01N NaOH, 0.1N NaOH and distilled water.

Apparatus: Separating funnel(250ml),conical flask ,pipette, burette, stoppered bottle,

PRINCIPLE:

When a solute is shaken with two immiscible solvents it gets distributed between the solvents. This distribution of solute in two solvents depends on the solubility of the solute in two solvents. At the distribution equilibrium, the ratio of concentration of the solute in the two solvents is constant at a given temperature. The constant is called partition coefficient (K) or the distribution coefficient of the solute between the two solvents.

PROCEDURE:

Prepared the following mixtures in separating funnels:

Set I: 25ml water + 25ml of saturated solution of benzoic acid in benzene.

Set II: 25ml water + 20 ml saturated solution of benzoic acid in benzene + 5ml benzene.

Set III: 25ml water + 15ml saturated solution of benzoic acid in benzene + 10ml benzene.

Shaken the mixture in the separating funnel vigorously for about 30 minutes so that the benzoic acid gets distributed between the two solvents and the distribution equilibrium is reached. Allowed the flasks to stand for 10 minutes to separate into two clear layers (removed the stopper of the separating funnel and keep its mouth open during this period to facilitate the separation). Drain off the lower aqueous layers in 3 different stoppered dry bottles. (Discard the intermediate layer between the two phases).Benzene layer remains in the separating funnels. Using a dry pipette take 5ml of organic layer (Benzene) into a conical flask containing 10ml of water and titrate against 0.1N NaOH using Phenolphthalein as an indicator. The end point is indicated by the color change from colorless to pink. Pipette out 10ml of the aqueous layer using dry pipette and titrate it against NaOH solution using phenolphthalein as an indicator. End point is indicated by the color change from colorless to pink.

OBSERVATION TABLE:

Set No.	Vorg	Vaq	Norg = Corg	Naq = Caq	K	logCorg	log Caq

Mean partition coefficient (K) =

Where,

V_{org} = Volume in ml of 0.1N Sodium hydroxide per 5ml of organic layer

N_{aq} = Volume in ml of 0.1N Sodium hydroxide per 5ml of aqueous layer

N_{org} = Normality of organic layer

N_{aq} = Normality of aqueous layer

C_{org} = Concentration of organic layer in g mole/lit

C_{aq} = Concentration of aqueous layer in g mole/lit

$K = C_{aq}/ (C_{org})1/2$ = Partition coefficient of benzoic acid in water and benzene.

CALCULATIONS

Set I:

1. For organic layer

Normality of NaOH (N1=0.1N)

Volume of Organic layer pipetted (V2) = 5ml

N1V1 (Sodium hydroxide) = N2V2 (Organic layer)

$$N2 = \frac{0.1 \times V1}{5} = N_{org}$$

Similarly calculate concentration of benzoic acid in organic layer of sets II and III

2. For aqueous layer

Normality of NaOH (N1=0.01N)

Volume of aqueous layer pipetted (V2) = 5ml

N1V1 (Sodium hydroxide) = N2V2 (aqueous layer)

$$N2 = \frac{0.1 \times V1}{5} = N_{aq}$$

Similarly calculate concentration of benzoic acid in aqueous layer of sets II and III

Graph

Plot the graph of log C_{aq} Vs log C_{org}

$$\text{Partition coefficient } (K) = \frac{C_{aq}}{C_{org}^{1/2}}$$

log C_{aq} = 1/n log C_{org} + log K

Above equation is equation of a straight line (y = mx +c)

Result from graph

Slope (m) =1/n

Therefore, n is nearly =

Substituting the value of slope of line in the equation log

C_{aq} = 1/n log C_{org}+ log K

log C_{aq} = log C_{org} + log K

log K =

K =

Result:

1. Partition coefficient of benzoic acid between distilled water and benzene is...................... by calculation and ....by graph.
2. Since $C_{aq}/ C_{org}^{1/2}$ is practically constant benzoic acid exists as a dimer (n=2) in benzene.
3. Molecular condition of benzoic acid in benzene is 1/slope = n = ... ,molecules of benzoic acid associate in benzene.